BIN DOES THIS GO IN? AM I USING TOO MUCH [...] JOEY OR A C[...]
THIS COFFEE SHOP? DO I HAVE TO ASK FOR THE [...] PE[...]
S BAD FOR YOU? IS ANYTHING GOOD FOR YOU? [...] IS [...]
VE I HAD TOO MUCH COFFEE? IS THAT WHY MY HANDWRITING IS SO
C ATTACK? AM I BEING PRODUCTIVE? WHAT AM I GOING TO EAT? TAK[...]
? SHOULD I GET RID OF EVERYTHING? WHERE ARE MY HAIR TIES? WHE[...]
? DID I LEAVE THE IRON ON? SHOULD I EAT THE REST OR SAVE I[...]
BRUNCH? HOW SHOULD WE SPLIT THIS? SHOULD WE GET ICE CREA[...]
GETTING FIRED? SHOULD I BE MY OWN BOSS? IS THIS A HEAL[...]
START THIS EMAIL? CAN YOU TELL I'M STRESSED? WHAT DOES[...]
ORE? DO YOU HAVE ANY DIETARY RESTRICTIONS? WHAT CAN I S[...]
ER TO TALK ABOUT? SHOULD I WASH MY HANDS AGAIN? AM I A G[...]
CT OR EFFECT? IS THIS OFF TOPIC? SHOULD I HAVE ANOTHER[...]
MY BOOK IF YOU READ IN THE BATHTUB? WHY DO I CARE ABO[...]
IGHT? AM I CATASTROPHIZING? DO PEOPLE REALLY DISAGREE [...]
NANGE ANYONE'S MIND? AM I DOING ENOUGH? HOW ARE YOUR HO[...]
LEARNED IN SCHOOL? WILL I EVER USE THE MATH I LEARNED[...]
? DO I ALREADY KNOW THE ANSWER TO THAT? CAN I KEEP I[...]
ASSES? AM I FLOSSING ENOUGH? SHOULD I POP THIS ZIT? JUS[...]
MUCH CHEESE? HOW AM I FULL ALREADY? CHIPS? GUAC? HOW [...]
RE? WHERE ARE MY HAIR TIES? CAN WE HANDLE A TRIP[...]
HIS A DEAL BREAKER? SHOULD WE TALK? AM I WRONG AB[...]
YEAR? HOW DO I GET THROUGH ANOTHER HARSH WINTER?[...]
ON TV? CHIPS FOR DINNER? WHERE'S MY WALLET? DD[...]
GETTING ANYTHING? HAS ANYONE SEEN KEVIN? DOES EVER[...]
ARE THE INGREDIENTS IN A MARSHMALLOW? HOW FAR CA[...]
DO FOR MY BIRTHDAY? WHAT IF NOBODY CAN MAKE IT? [...]
NDLE? SHOULD I ADD ANOTHER CUP TO THE COLLECTION ON[...]
MATION POINTS? SHOULD I SPEAK UP? AM I A PERFECTIONI[...]
SHOULD I REGIFT THIS WINE? WHAT DID WE DECIDE AB[...]
NEUROTIC BOOKS? NEUROTICA? IS THAT DUMB? ARE YOU JUD[...]

AM I OVERTHINKING THIS?

ōō

AM I OVERTHINKING THIS?

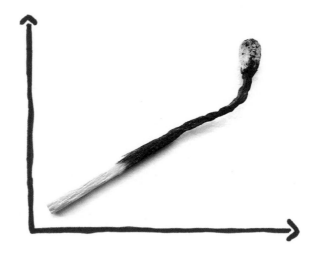

OVER-ANSWERING LIFE'S QUESTIONS IN 101 CHARTS

by MICHELLE RIAL

CHRONICLE BOOKS
SAN FRANCISCO

Library of Congress Cataloging-in-Publication Data

Names: Rial, Michelle, author.

Title: Am I overthinking this? / by Michelle Rial.

Description: San Francisco : Chronicle Books, [2019]

Identifiers: LCCN 2018035784 | ISBN 9781452175867 (hardcover : alk. paper)

Subjects: LCSH: Worry--Humor.

Classification: LCC PN6231.W648 R53 2019 | DDC 818/.602--dc23 LC record available
at https://lccn.loc.gov/2018035784

Manufactured in China.

Design by Rachel Harrell.

Amtrak is a registered trademark of National Railroad Passenger Corporation. The Beatles is a
registered trademark of Apple Corps Limited. Disneyland is a registered trademark of Disney
Enterprises, Inc. IKEA is a registered trademark of Inter IKEA Systems B.V. Kryptonite is a
registered trademark of Schlage Lock Company LLC. La Croix is a registered trademark of
Everfresh Beverages, Inc. Teflon is a registered trademark of The Chemours Company FC, LLC.
Q-tip is a registered trademark of Unilever. Walt Disney World is a registered trademark of Disney
Enterprises, Inc.

10 9 8 7 6

Chronicle books and gifts are available at special quantity discounts to corporations,
professional associations, literacy programs, and other organizations. For details and discount
information, please contact our corporate/premiums department at
corporatesales@chroniclebooks.com or at 1-800-759-0190.

Chronicle Books LLC
680 Second Street
San Francisco, California 94107
www.chroniclebooks.com

100% OF THIS BOOK IS
DEDICATED TO LENNY

THE OTHER 100% IS
FOR MY PARENTS

Table of Contents

Introduction

This is not a book of charts.

This is a book of questions. Questions I'll attempt to answer and over-answer with the help of charts, graphs, and physical objects. Questions like: Which wine should I bring? How should I start this email? Do I *really* need more plants?

This book is a window into my anxieties, and maybe some of yours, too. In it, I try to capture the infinite mind maps we, as over-thinkers, create when we attempt to make even the most insignificant of decisions.

This book has dreams of being on your coffee table, but hopefully never as a coaster (more about book lending etiquette on page 69). It dreams of being a gift to your friend with the plant ~~problem~~ hobby. It hopes to be a reminder that there isn't always one right answer—and that, sometimes, the only answer is to pick a path and keep moving.

This book is a work-around. It's a response to a long struggle with chronic pain that eventually limited my ability to work as a graphic designer. I'd spent years creating dense digital charts and infographics, accompanied by an endless cycle of flare-ups. I eventually left my job as a senior designer at a fun media company with great snacks, very aware of all that I could no longer do. Eventually, and thankfully, I shifted my focus to what I *could* do—charts—but they had to be simple. I switched to pen and paper, adding the occasional object when my hands were too achy from drawing. With these simple charts, I could tell the story of my many anxieties in just a few lines.

This book didn't cure me, but it did give me a reason to keep going.

But maybe I'm overthinking it.

It's also a book of charts.

OVERTHINKING

My Daily Routine

WHERE ARE MY HAIR TIES?

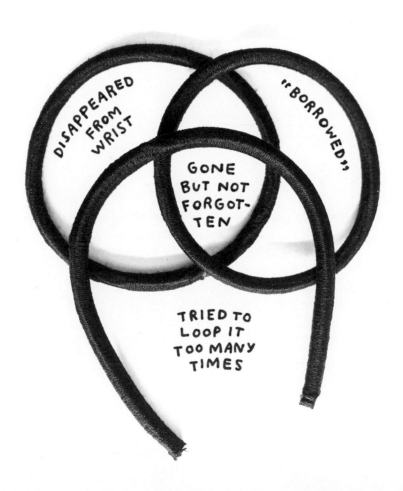

DISAPPEARED FROM WRIST

"BORROWED"

GONE BUT NOT FORGOT-TEN

TRIED TO LOOP IT TOO MANY TIMES

DO I HAVE ENOUGH HAIRPINS?

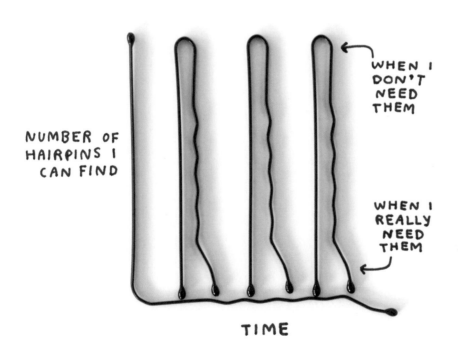

NUMBER OF
HAIRPINS I
CAN FIND

WHEN I
DON'T
NEED
THEM

WHEN I
REALLY
NEED
THEM

TIME

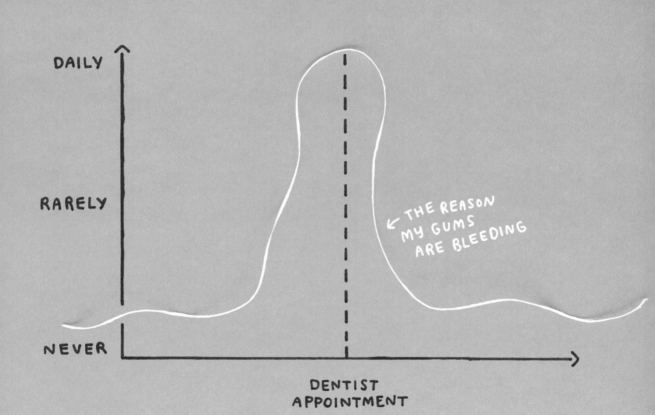

HOW LONG SHOULD THIS DISH SOAK?

TOTAL SOAKING TIME

A

B

A NECESSARY SOAKING TIME

B OOPS, I FORGOT ABOUT IT

WEARING
SHOES
INSIDE

LAUNDROMAT
CARTS

WATER
PARKS

DRINKING
FOUNTAIN

OTHER PEOPLE'S KID

HAVING
A PET

SHOPPING
CARTS

SALONS

OTHER
PEOPLE'S
PETS

AN
OLD
JAR
OF PEANUT
BUTTER

CROSSWALK
BUTTONS

LUGGAGE
ON A BED

REST
STOPS

SHOULD I WASH
MY HANDS AGAIN?

DOUBLE-

MY
OWN
PHONE

SHARING
ANYTHING

SHAKING
HANDS

MY DOG
LICKING
ME IN
THE EYE

TOILET
HANDLE

DECORATIVE
HOTEL PILLOW

FREE
SAMPLES

DRINK
LIDS

DISNEY
WORLD
AND LAND

S
CL
C

THE
POOL

PAPER
TOWEL
DISPENSER

WALKING
BAREFOOT

THE GYM

THE
OCEAN

MAIL

GERMS ─────────────

PUBLIC
TRANSIT

BATHTUBS

PAWS

PANTS

TAKING
OUT THE
TRASH

ALL AREAS
OF THE
AIRPORT

FEET

THE AREA
UNDER
THE SINK

THE DOO
HANDLE A
YOU'VE AL
WASHED

THE
POST
OFFICE

THE DMV

NAIL
SALONS

WATER
FOUNTAINS

A POORLY
LABELED
DISTINCTION
BETWEEN USED
SPOONS AND
CLEAN SPOONS

THE OUTSIDE
OF A BOTTLE
OF HAND
SANITIZER

E-READERS

MOVIE
THEATER
SEATS

TH
ZO

THE
BUFFET
LINE

THE
LIBRARY

BAR
NUTS

DOORKNOBS

DUST

NAIL
CLIPPERS

CONTACT
LENS CASE

EATING

UNTIED
SHOELACES

PLAYING
CARDS

TRYING
ON A
BATHING
SUIT

PORTA-
POTTY
WALLS

HAIR

SUITCASE
WHEELS

SOMEONE WITH "ALLERGIES"

A LOOSE
COUGH

SNEEZE
CLOUD

VAPING

WHEN YOUR PILLOW
FALLS ON THE FLOOR

BACKPACKS

THE
BUS

FLIES

GERMS

UBER

LAPTOP
FAN

ALUMINUM
CAN

WHATEVER
A "WATER
BUG" IS

DISH
TOWELS

HAND
TOWELS

BAR OF
SOAP

YOGA
MATS

ROLLER
COASTERS

JURY
DUTY

BABIES

CABS

KEYBOARD

WET
DRAINS

FLIP
FLOPS

BIKE
SHARE

MOVING TRUCK
MOVING TOWARD
YOU

SCHOOL
BUS

PUBLIC
SHOWERS

MOUSE

THE BATHROOM
FLOOR

GERMS

BIKE
TIRES

THE BOTTOM
OF A TOTE BAG

GAS
STATIONS

TSA
BINS

MONEY

PIGEONS

DISHES
LEFT
TO "SOAK"

THE OFFICE
KITCHEN

PLUNGERS

QUILTS

STAIR
RAILINGS

OTHER
BIRDS

DIRTY
HANDS

USED
HATS

THE
MALL

MAGAZINES
AT THE DOCTOR'S
OFFICE

AIRPLANE
TRAY TABLE

CUPS PLACED
UPSIDE DOWN

SITTING
ON THE
FLOOR

RUGS

GERMS

BOARD
GAMES

FLIP
CUP

AMTRAK

BOWLING
BALL FINGER
HOLES

A PASSED
BLUNT

BEER
PONG

COLLEGE
IN GENERAL

CAST-
IRON
PAN

ELEVATOR
BUTTONS

MAKEUP
TESTERS

STICKY
FLOORS

ANY TYPE
OF BONG

THE UNDERSIDE
OF A PICNIC BLANKET

WEIGHTS

WHAT DOES MY TOTE BAG SAY ABOUT ME?

I WANT YOU TO KNOW WHAT I CARE ABOUT

I CARE ABOUT REDUCING WASTE

I CARE ABOUT INDEPENDENT BOOKSTORES (ESPECIALLY IF THE LOGO IS NICE)

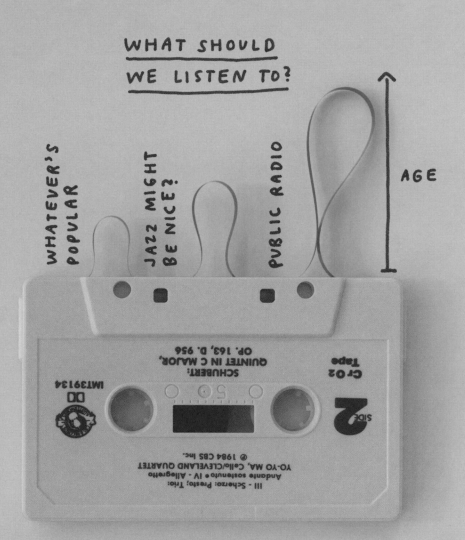

HAS ANYONE SEEN MY SUNGLASSES?

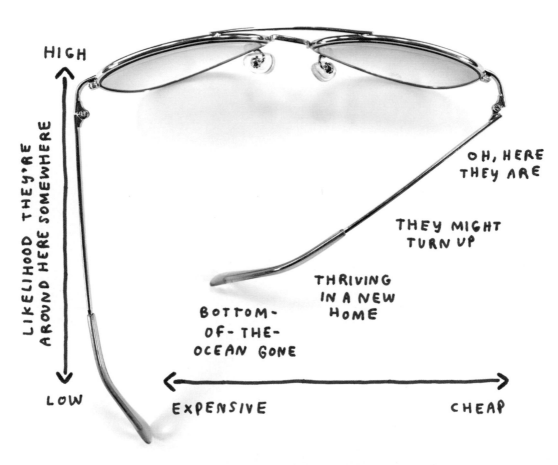

OH, HERE THEY ARE

THEY MIGHT TURN UP

THRIVING IN A NEW HOME

BOTTOM-OF-THE-OCEAN GONE

LIKELIHOOD THEY'RE AROUND HERE SOMEWHERE

HIGH

LOW

EXPENSIVE

CHEAP

DO I NEED TO CANCEL MY CREDIT CARDS?

I CAN'T FIND
MY WALLET

FINALLY
MEMORIZED
THE CVC

IT WAS IN
MY JACKET
ALL ALONG!

CANCEL
EVERYTHING

GOT MY
NEW CARDS

CAN I INJURE MYSELF
WHILE Q-TIPPING?

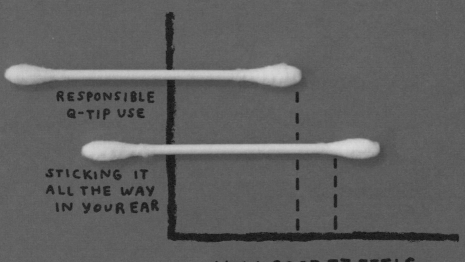

RESPONSIBLE
Q-TIP USE

STICKING IT
ALL THE WAY
IN YOUR EAR

HOW GOOD IT FEELS

SHOULD I POP *this* ZIT?

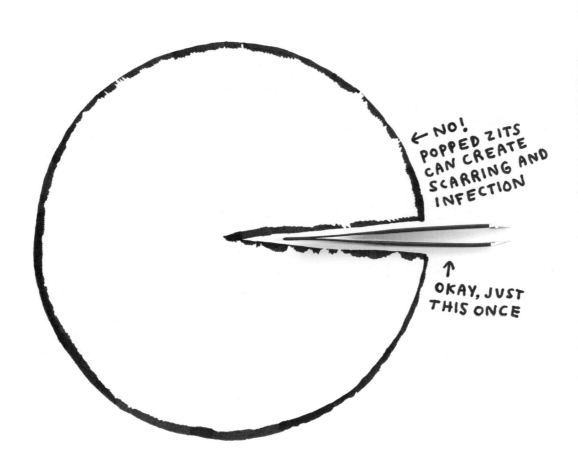

← NO! POPPED ZITS CAN CREATE SCARRING AND INFECTION

↑ OKAY, JUST THIS ONCE

DID I LEAVE THE IRON ON?

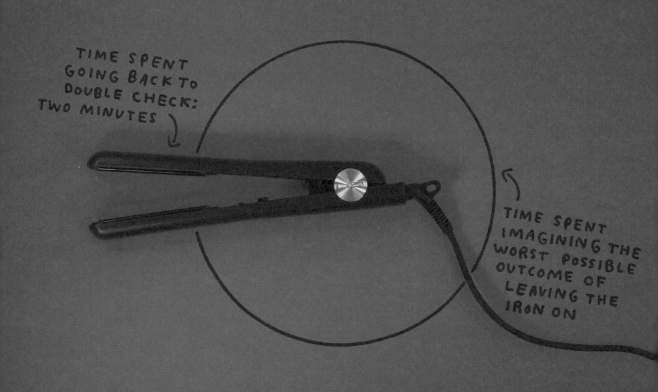

TIME SPENT
GOING BACK TO
DOUBLE CHECK:
TWO MINUTES

TIME SPENT
IMAGINING THE
WORST POSSIBLE
OUTCOME OF
LEAVING THE
IRON ON

WHAT AM I FORGETTING?

I'M GOING OUT

KEYS
PHONE WALLET

I'M WALKING THE DOG

KEYS
PHONE WALLET
BAGS (FOR POOP)

I'M TRAVELING INTERNATIONALLY

PASSPORT
KEYS
PHONE
WALLET
BAGS
(NOT FOR POOP)

I'M TRAVELING TO PARIS WITH THE McCALLISTERS

KEVIN!!!

LIKELIHOOD OF LEAVING IT BEHIND

OVERTHINKING

Breakfast, Lunch, and Dinner

IS THIS WINE OK ?

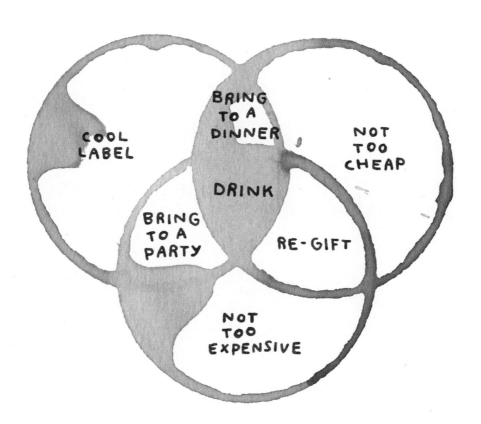

COOL LABEL

BRING TO A DINNER

NOT TOO CHEAP

DRINK

BRING TO A PARTY

RE-GIFT

NOT TOO EXPENSIVE

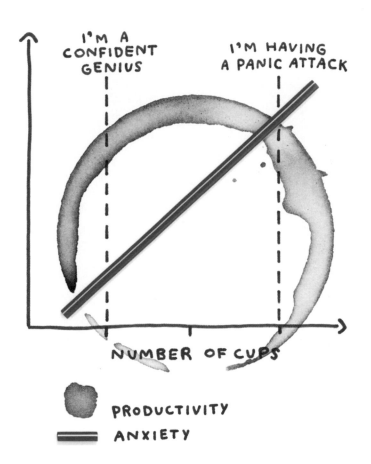

SHOULD I HAVE MORE COFFEE?

I'M A CONFIDENT GENIUS

I'M HAVING A PANIC ATTACK

NUMBER OF CUPS

PRODUCTIVITY

ANXIETY

AM I EATING
TOO MUCH CHEESE?

I HAVE
A HEALTHY
RELATIONSHIP
WITH CHEESE

I HAVE A
PROBLEM

GIVING UP
CHEESE
WOULD BE
A BRIE-ZE

I'M A
SOCIAL
EATER

ALL FOOD
IS A VEHICLE
FOR CHEESE

I'M
VERY
SICK

SHOULD I GRAB SOME KALE?

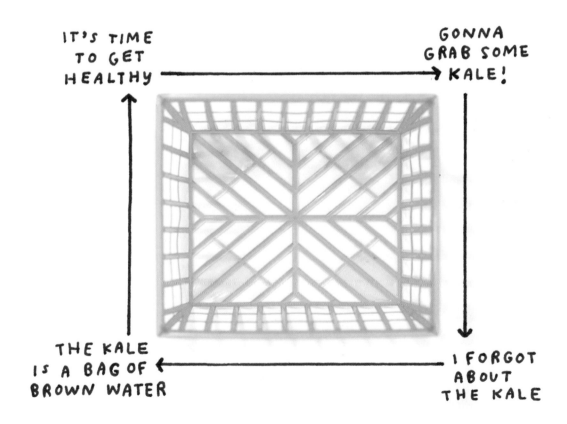

IT'S TIME TO GET HEALTHY

GONNA GRAB SOME KALE!

THE KALE IS A BAG OF BROWN WATER

I FORGOT ABOUT THE KALE

HOW AM I FULL ALREADY?

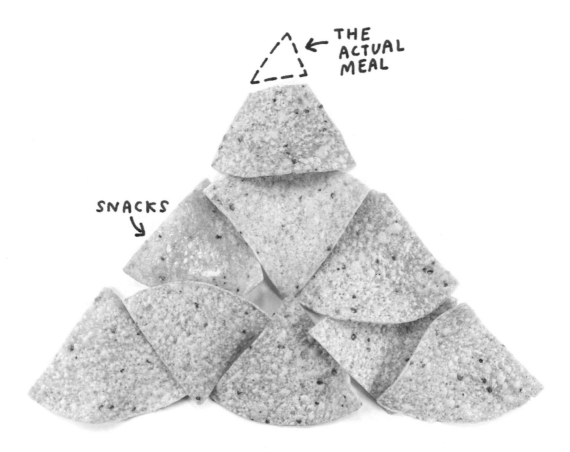

THE ACTUAL MEAL

SNACKS

A FOOD PYRAMID FOR SNACKERS

DOES THIS NEED BUTTER?

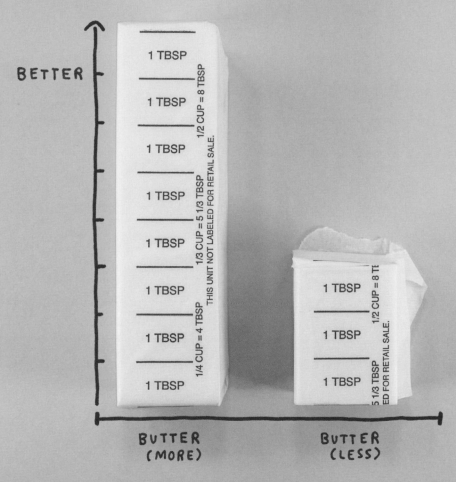

SHOULD WE GET ICE CREAM?

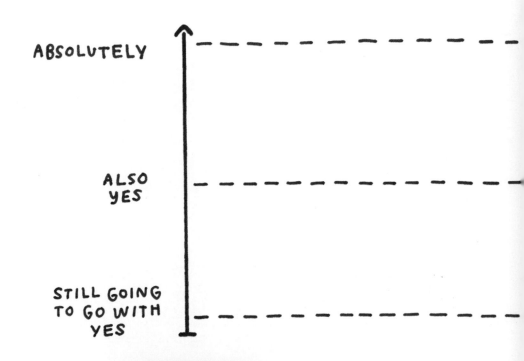

ABSOLUTELY

ALSO YES

STILL GOING TO GO WITH YES

LIKELIHOOD OF ICE CREAM RUN

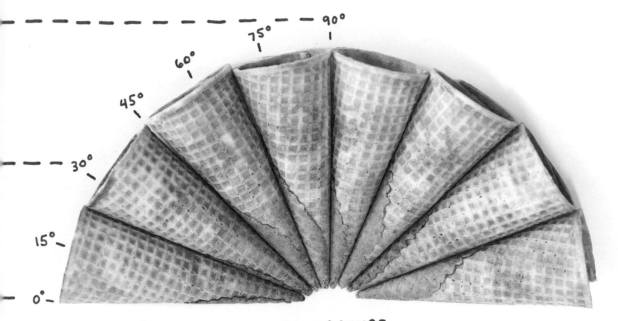

TEMPERATURE
IN FAHRENHEIT

37

HOW SHOULD WE SPLIT THIS?

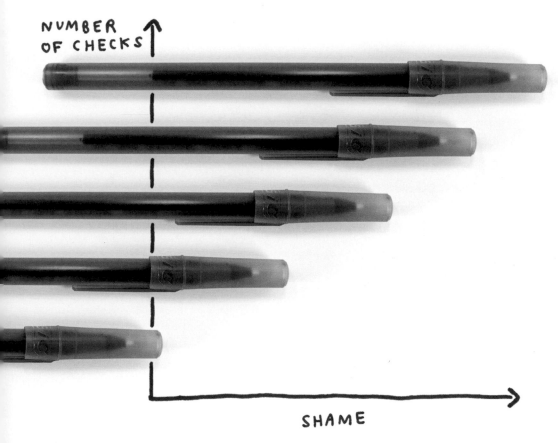

NUMBER
OF CHECKS

SHAME

IS BRUNCH FISCALLY IRRESPONSIBLE?

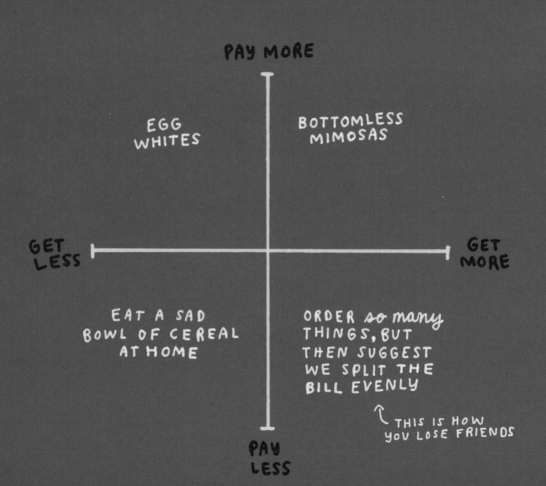

IS IT WATERMELON SEASON?

NORTHERN HEMISPHERE

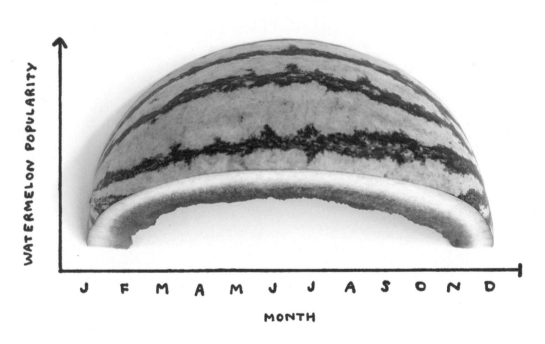

WATERMELON POPULARITY

J F M A M J J A S O N D

MONTH

IS IT WATERMELON SEASON?

SOUTHERN HEMISPHERE

WATERMELON POPULARITY

J F M A M J J A S O N D

MONTH

WHY DO I FEEL TERRIBLE?

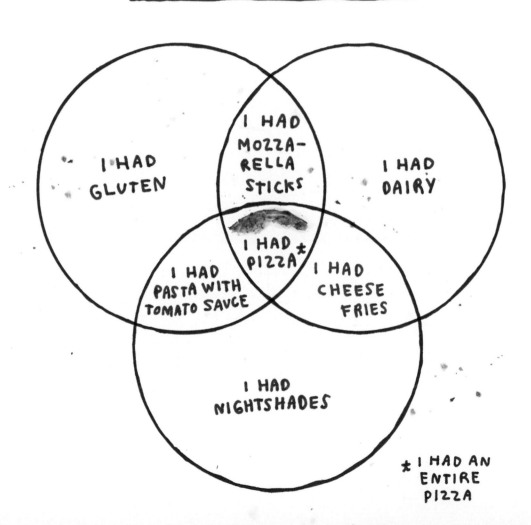

I HAD GLUTEN

I HAD MOZZA-RELLA STICKS

I HAD DAIRY

I HAD PIZZA *

I HAD PASTA WITH TOMATO SAUCE

I HAD CHEESE FRIES

I HAD NIGHTSHADES

* I HAD AN ENTIRE PIZZA

SHOULD I EAT THE REST OR SAVE IT?

IF I SAVE HALF, I'LL HAVE A WHOLE MEAL FOR LATER

JUST A FEW MORE BITES

FORGET IT

STILL OR SPARKLING?

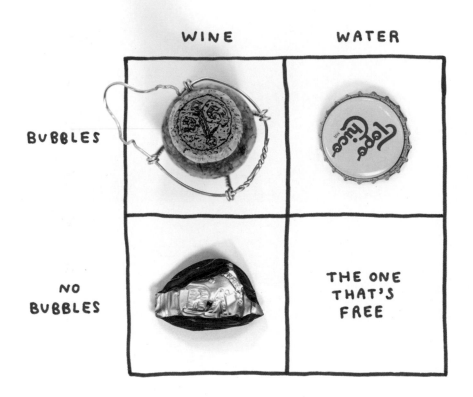

WINE   WATER

BUBBLES

NO BUBBLES   THE ONE THAT'S FREE

WHAT CAN I SERVE AT THIS PARTY?

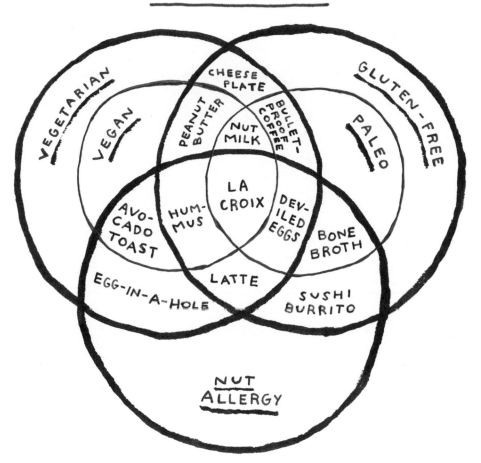

VEGETARIAN

VEGAN

GLUTEN-FREE

PALEO

CHEESE PLATE

PEANUT BUTTER

NUT MILK

BULLET-PROOF COFFEE

LA CROIX

AVO-CADO TOAST

HUM-MUS

DEV-ILED EGGS

BONE BROTH

EGG-IN-A-HOLE

LATTE

SUSHI BURRITO

NUT ALLERGY

OVERTHINKING

the Subject Line

HOW SHOULD I START THIS EMAIL?

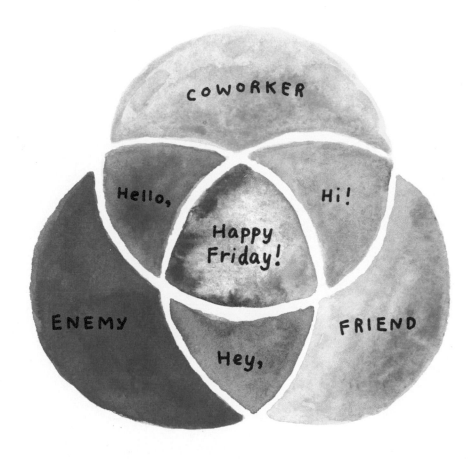

COWORKER

Hello,

Hi!

Happy Friday!

ENEMY

FRIEND

Hey,

TIP: SAVE ALL YOUR EMAILS FOR FRIDAY

HOW SHOULD I END THIS EMAIL?

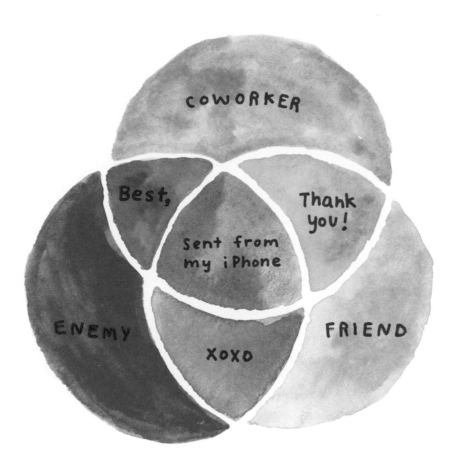

COWORKER

Best,

Thank you!

Sent from my iPhone

ENEMY

XOXO

FRIEND

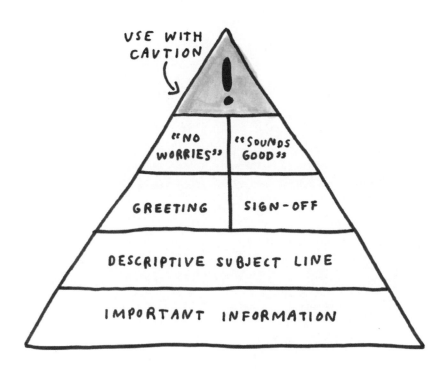

DOES THIS NEED AN EXCLAMATION POINT?

USE WITH CAUTION

!

"NO WORRIES" "SOUNDS GOOD"

GREETING SIGN-OFF

DESCRIPTIVE SUBJECT LINE

IMPORTANT INFORMATION

EMAIL STRUCTURE PYRAMID

AM I GETTING FIRED?

THEY SAID...	IT MIGHT MEAN	BUT IT PROBABLY MEANS
SOUNDS GOOD!	EVERYTHING IS FINE	EVERYTHING IS FINE
SOUNDS GOOD.		SOUNDS GOOD.
THAT'S FINE.	I'M GETTING FIRED	IT'S FINE.
OK.		OK.
HMMM...		HMMM...
HEY, CAN WE TALK?	WOW, MAYBE I'M REALLY GETTING FIRED??	:(

ARE PEOPLE JUDGING ME BY MY DESK?

IT'S MESSY | IT'S NEAT

IT'S QUIRKY

YOU'RE THE CREATIVE TYPE

YOU'RE IMPORTANT

IT'S MINIMAL

YOU'RE AT HAPPY HOUR

YOU'RE STORING A LOT OF RESENTMENT IN THOSE DRAWERS

WHAT IF I WATCH OLD EPISODES OF "THE OFFICE" WHILE I WORK?

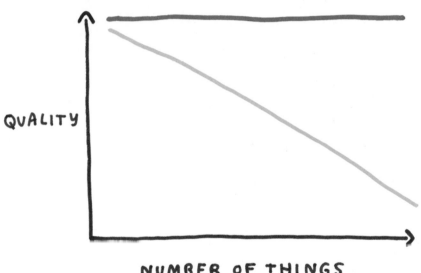

QUALITY

NUMBER OF THINGS
YOU'RE DOING* AT ONCE

● EXPECTATION
● REALITY

* THAT'S WHAT
SHE SAID

WHAT IF I FAIL?

	FAILURES	SUCCESSES
MANY ATTEMPTS	~~IIII~~ ~~IIII~~ ~~IIII~~ ~~IIII~~ ~~IIII~~ ~~IIII~~ ~~IIII~~ ~~IIII~~ ~~IIII~~ ~~IIII~~ ~~IIII~~ ~~IIII~~	~~IIII~~
NO ATTEMPTS	NONE	N/A

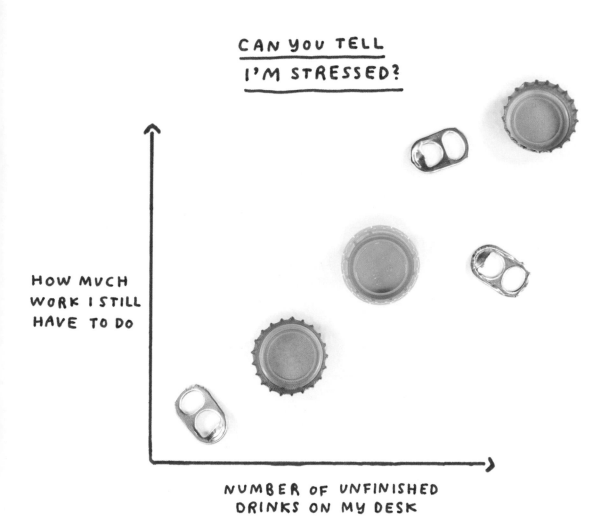

AM I GOOD
AT MY JOB?

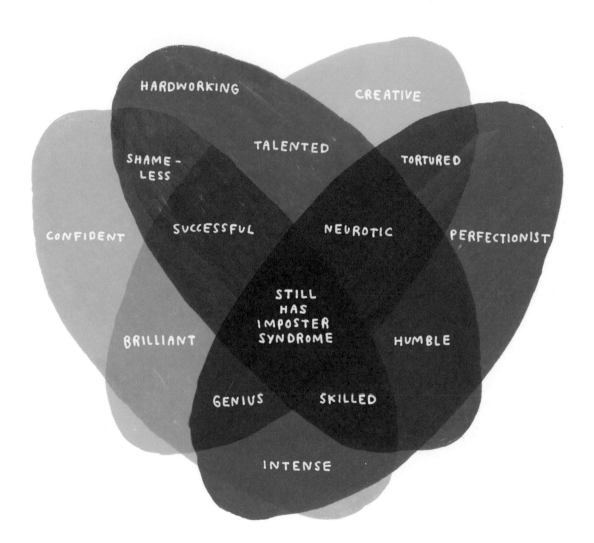

HARDWORKING

CREATIVE

TALENTED

SHAME-
LESS

TORTURED

CONFIDENT

SUCCESSFUL

NEUROTIC

PERFECTIONIST

STILL
HAS
IMPOSTER
SYNDROME

BRILLIANT

HUMBLE

GENIUS

SKILLED

INTENSE

WHAT'S MORE IMPORTANT?

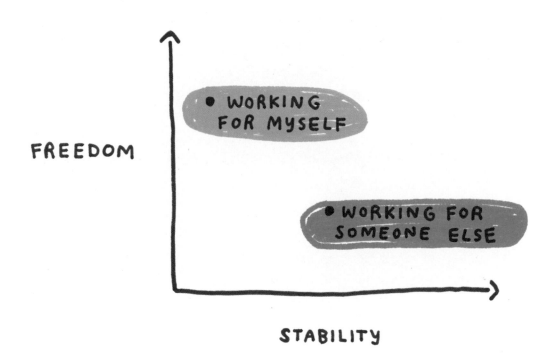

IS THIS A
HEALTHY LIFESTYLE?

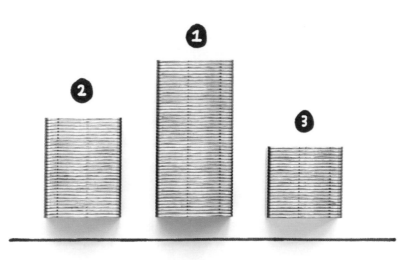

2 BIKES TO WORK

1 ACTUALLY STANDS AT STANDING DESK

3 MULTIPLE TRIPS TO THE FRIDGE

CORPORATE OLYMPICS

HOW DO I MAKE SMALL TALK?

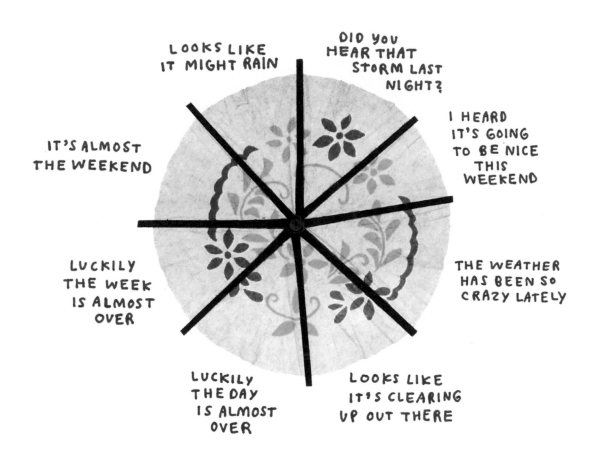

LOOKS LIKE IT MIGHT RAIN

DID YOU HEAR THAT STORM LAST NIGHT?

I HEARD IT'S GOING TO BE NICE THIS WEEKEND

IT'S ALMOST THE WEEKEND

THE WEATHER HAS BEEN SO CRAZY LATELY

LUCKILY THE WEEK IS ALMOST OVER

LUCKILY THE DAY IS ALMOST OVER

LOOKS LIKE IT'S CLEARING UP OUT THERE

DO WE HAVE ANYTHING BETTER TO TALK ABOUT?

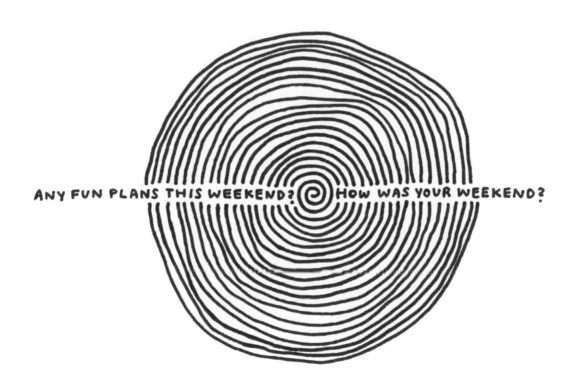

ANY FUN PLANS THIS WEEKEND? HOW WAS YOUR WEEKEND?

OVERTHINKING

Adult Life

IS IT NORMAL TO CRY ON YOUR BIRTHDAY?

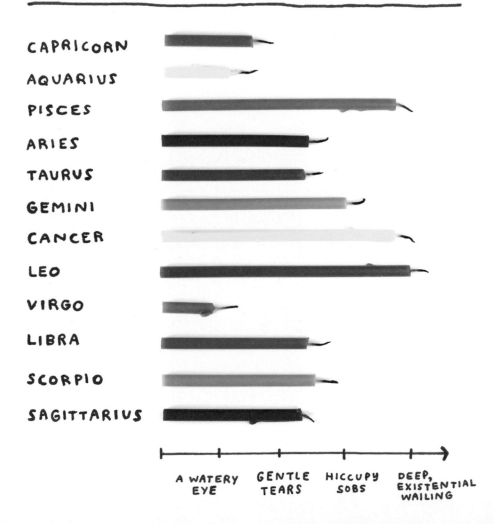

CAPRICORN

AQUARIUS

PISCES

ARIES

TAURUS

GEMINI

CANCER

LEO

VIRGO

LIBRA

SCORPIO

SAGITTARIUS

A WATERY EYE   GENTLE TEARS   HICCUPY SOBS   DEEP, EXISTENTIAL WAILING

WHAT SHOULD I DO FOR MY BIRTHDAY?

ARCHIVE BIRTHDAY EMAIL FROM MY OLD DENTIST

WATCH THE SOCIAL MEDIA NOTIFICATIONS ROLL IN

PANIC

NOTHING

EAT TRENDY ALTERNATIVE TO CAKE

NOTHING, I MEAN IT

WEEP

PLAN A DINNER (NO WORRIES IF YOU CAN'T MAKE IT!)

I DON'T WANT ANYONE TO MAKE A BIG DEAL OUT OF IT, BUT A SMALL DEAL WOULD BE NICE

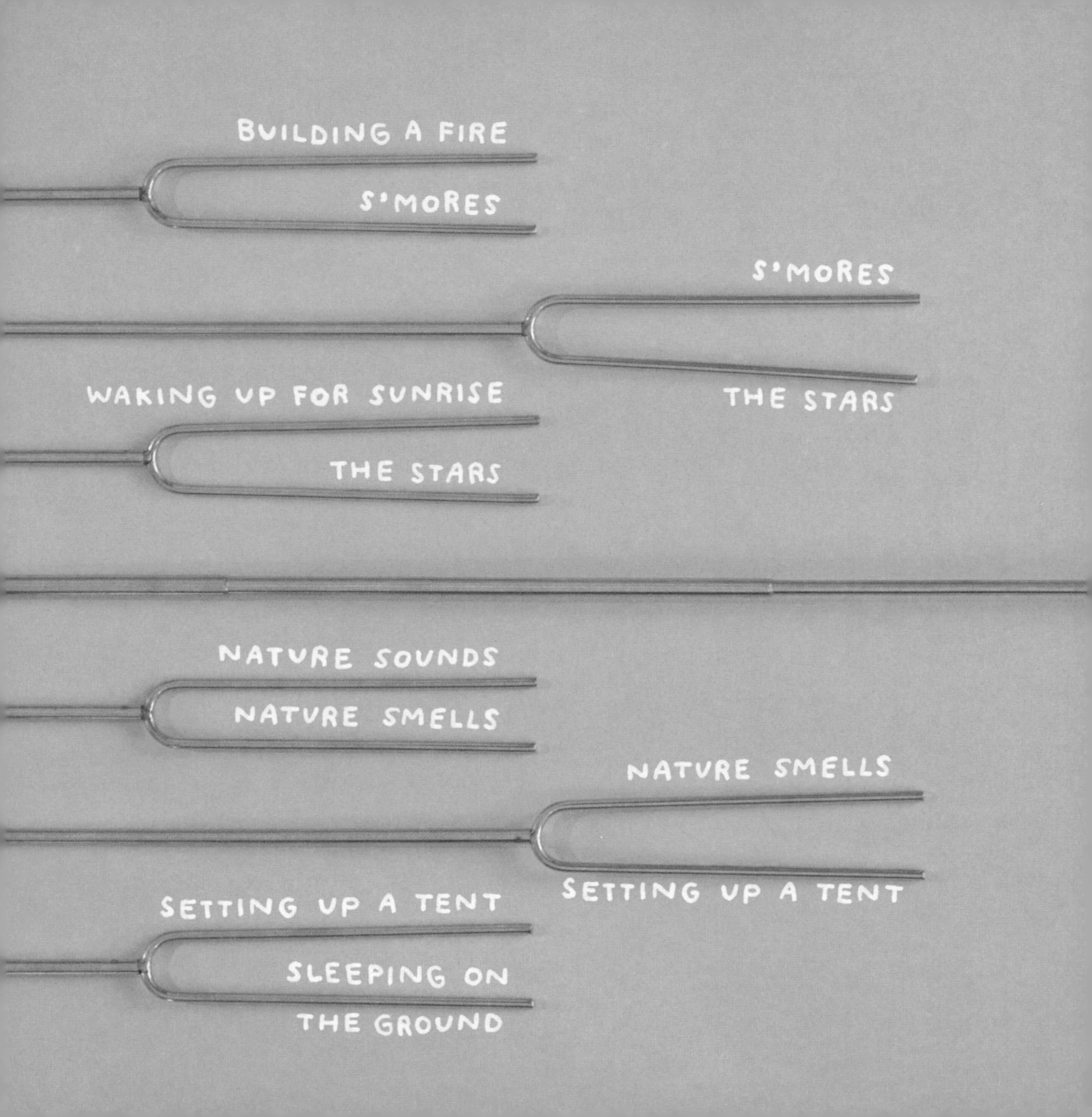

BUILDING A FIRE

S'MORES

S'MORES

WAKING UP FOR SUNRISE

THE STARS

THE STARS

NATURE SOUNDS

NATURE SMELLS

NATURE SMELLS

SETTING UP A TENT

SETTING UP A TENT

SLEEPING ON
THE GROUND

WHAT'S SO GREAT
ABOUT CAMPING?

S'MORES

NATURE SMELLS

IS THIS TOO LUXURIOUS?

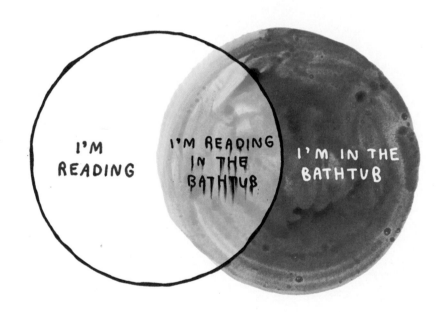

I'M READING

I'M READING IN THE BATHTUB

I'M IN THE BATHTUB

SHOULD I LEND YOU MY BOOKS?

LIKELIHOOD I'LL LEND YOU MY FAVORITE BOOK

← I CAN'T STAND THE IDEA THAT YOU HAVEN'T READ IT

← YOU USE A BOOKMARK

← YOU'RE A DOG-EAR-ER

← I'VE SEEN YOU USE A BOOK AS A COASTER

YOU READ
← IN THE BATHTUB

RISK

"He's trying to write
writing love stories. Bad
he'd let me. He writes th
just tell."

"Bad?"

"Substanceless."

"He's never been in l

"Probably not. Have

She nodded. She still

"Scrap thinks it mus
the stories."

"It is."

"I think it sounds nice."

"No." A thought edged its way out of her mouth. "You're substanceless, a little, I think."

SHOULD I GO OUT?

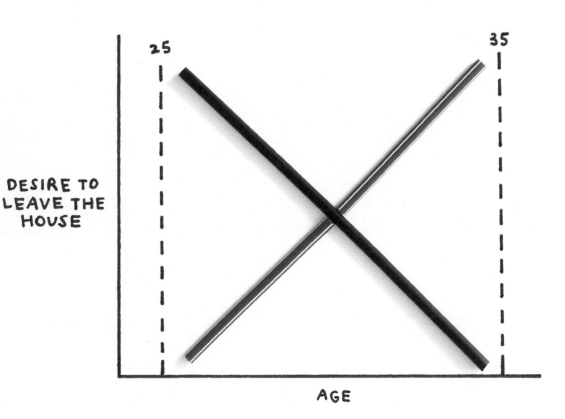

ON A FRIDAY NIGHT

ON A SATURDAY MORNING

WHAT AM I
GOING TO EAT?

ORDER
IN

EFFORT

GUILT

CHIPS AGAIN

FROZEN PIZZA

THE RECIPE I BOOKMARKED
THREE YEARS AGO

A FOOD PYRAMID FOR STAYING IN

CAN I KEEP IT ALIVE?

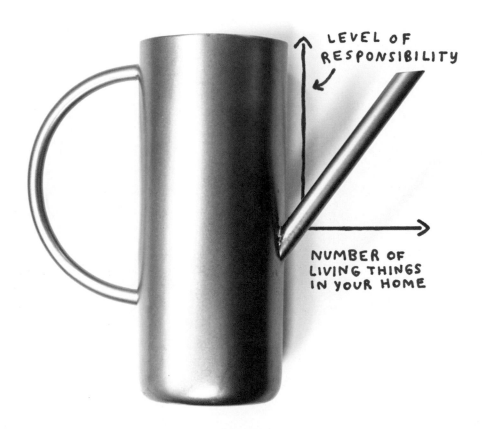

LEVEL OF
RESPONSIBILITY

NUMBER OF
LIVING THINGS
IN YOUR HOME

DO I HAVE TOO
MANY PLANTS*?

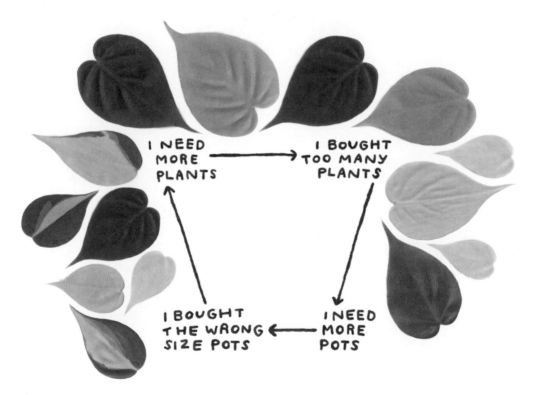

I NEED MORE PLANTS → I BOUGHT TOO MANY PLANTS

I BOUGHT THE WRONG SIZE POTS ← I NEED MORE POTS

*AND NOT LIKE, IN A "COOL URBAN JUNGLE" KIND OF WAY BUT IN AN UNHEALTHY, FIRE HAZARD KIND OF WAY?

WHICH WHITE PAINT
SHOULD I USE?

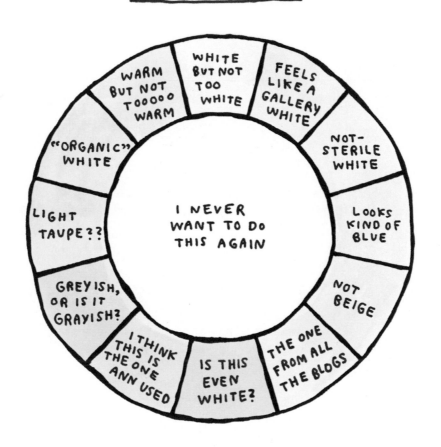

WARM BUT NOT TOOOOO WARM

WHITE BUT NOT TOO WHITE

FEELS LIKE A GALLERY WHITE

"ORGANIC" WHITE

NOT-STERILE WHITE

LIGHT TAUPE??

I NEVER WANT TO DO THIS AGAIN

LOOKS KIND OF BLUE

GREYISH, OR IS IT GRAYISH?

NOT BEIGE

I THINK THIS IS THE ONE ANN USED

IS THIS EVEN WHITE?

THE ONE FROM ALL THE BLOGS

WILL MY HOME PROJECT LOOK LIKE THE ONES I SEE ON TV?

SOMETHING WILL BE OVER BUDGET

SOMETHING WILL GO WRONG

PICK TWO
(BE REALISTIC)

TWO FUN-LOVING HOME RENOVATION EXPERTS WILL APPEAR

HOW DO I GET BETTER AT THIS?

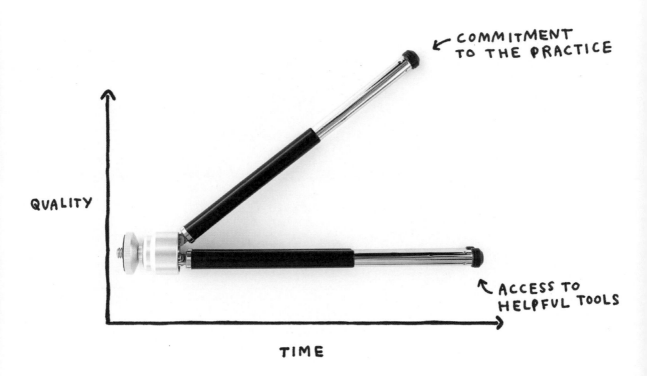

COMMITMENT TO THE PRACTICE

QUALITY

ACCESS TO HELPFUL TOOLS

TIME

IS IT TOO LATE TO START?

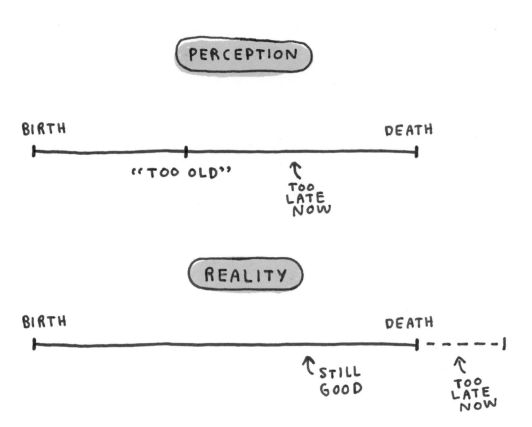

PERCEPTION

BIRTH ————————————|———————————— DEATH

"TOO OLD"

↑
TOO
LATE
NOW

REALITY

BIRTH ————————————————————— DEATH - - - - -|

↑ STILL
GOOD

↑
TOO
LATE
NOW

SHOULD I FRAME
THIS MYSELF?

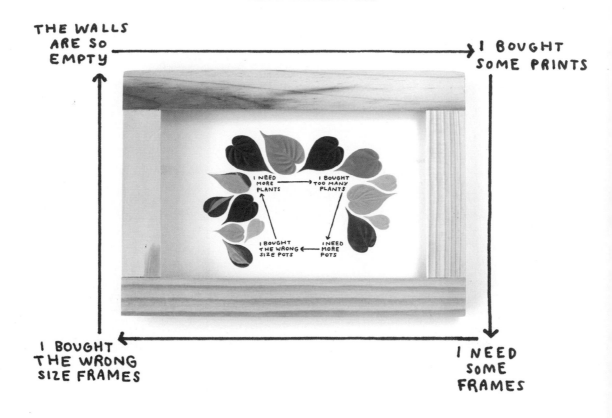

THE WALLS ARE SO EMPTY →

I BOUGHT SOME PRINTS

I NEED MORE PLANTS →

I BOUGHT TOO MANY PLANTS

I BOUGHT THE WRONG SIZE POTS ←

I NEED MORE POTS

I BOUGHT THE WRONG SIZE FRAMES ←

I NEED SOME FRAMES

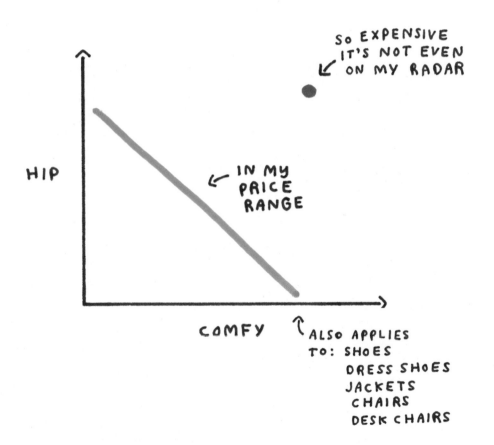

WHICH COUCH
SHOULD I GET?

SO EXPENSIVE
IT'S NOT EVEN
ON MY RADAR

HIP

IN MY
PRICE
RANGE

COMFY

ALSO APPLIES
TO: SHOES
    DRESS SHOES
    JACKETS
    CHAIRS
    DESK CHAIRS

DO I HAVE TO HAND-WASH THIS?

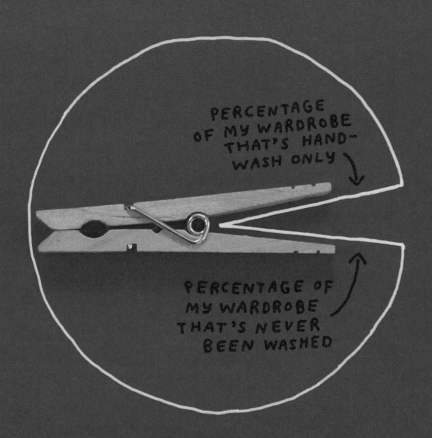

PERCENTAGE OF MY WARDROBE THAT'S HAND-WASH ONLY

PERCENTAGE OF MY WARDROBE THAT'S NEVER BEEN WASHED

TRIPS TO THE DRY CLEANER

WE ♥ OUR CUSTOMERS

J F M A M J J A S O N D

MONTH

SHOULD I BUY THIS?

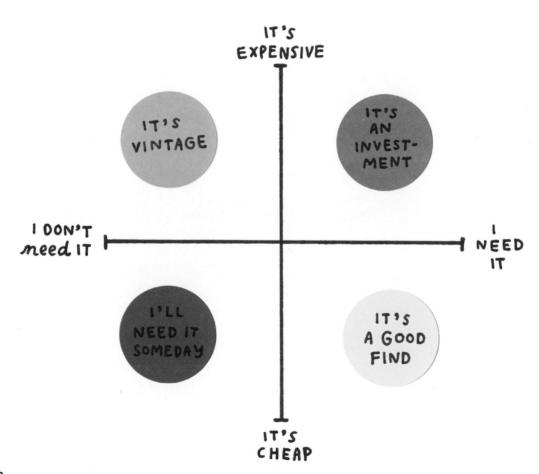

I'VE NEVER ONCE
WORN THIS HAT

HMM, EVEN
THIS HAT?

NO, I'LL
DEFINITELY
WEAR THIS

IT'S TIME TO
DECLUTTER
MY LIFE

ENTHUSIASM
FOR A MINIMALIST
LIFESTYLE

eventually

TIME

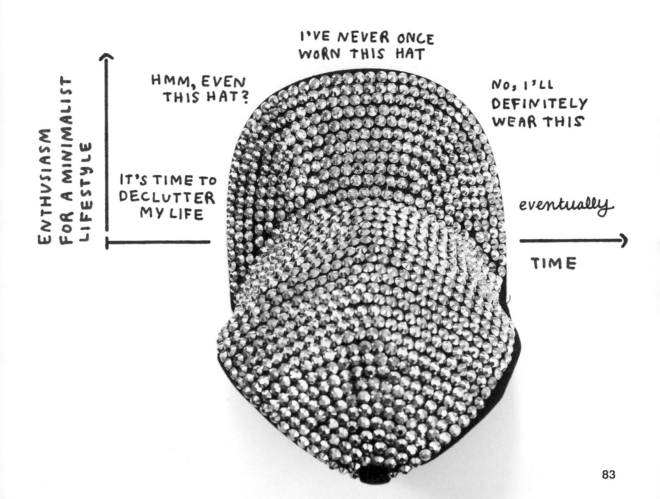

83

WHICH BIN DOES THIS GO IN?

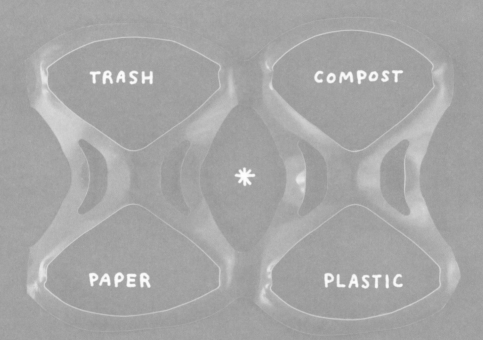

TRASH

COMPOST

*

PAPER

PLASTIC

* I'M NEVER ENTIRELY SURE,
BUT I do KNOW YOU HAVE
TO CUT THIS UP OR THE
DOLPHINS WILL GET HURT

AM I USING TOO MUCH PLASTIC?

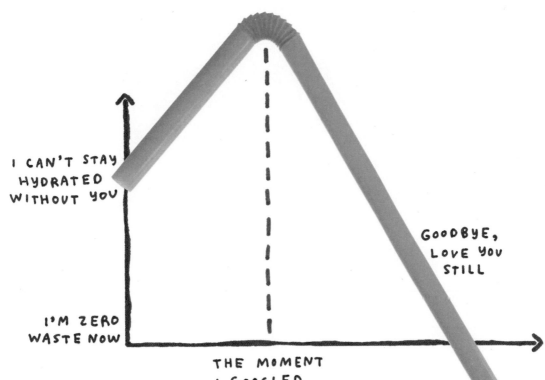

I CAN'T STAY
HYDRATED
WITHOUT YOU

GOODBYE,
LOVE YOU
STILL

I'M ZERO
WASTE NOW

THE MOMENT
I GOOGLED
THE TURTLES

OVERTHINKING

Relationships

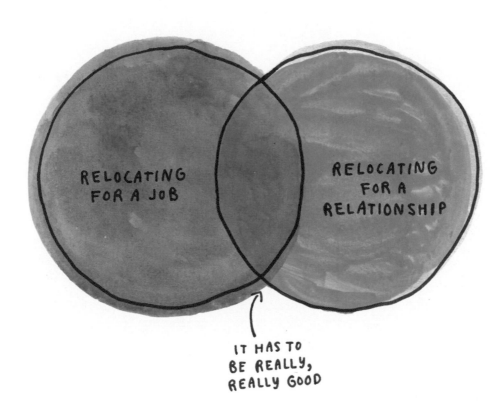

WILL OUR RELATIONSHIP
SURVIVE THIS STEP?

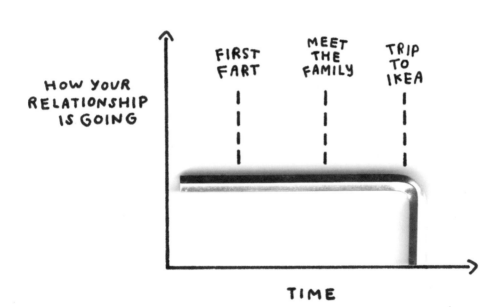

HOW YOUR
RELATIONSHIP
IS GOING

FIRST
FART

MEET
THE
FAMILY

TRIP
TO
IKEA

TIME

WHAT DOES THIS *mean* ?

THEY SAID...	IT MIGHT MEAN	BUT IT PROBABLY MEANS
THINGS ARE BUSY AT WORK	WORK IS SO BUSY RIGHT NOW	YOU'RE NOT A PRIORITY
I JUST GOT OUT OF A RELATIONSHIP	I'M READY FOR SOMETHING NEW	I STILL LOVE MY EX
I DON'T WANT TO PUT LABELS ON THIS	I'M EVOLVED AND MATURE	I'M KEEPING MY OPTIONS OPEN
MAYBE WE SHOULD PUT THIS ON PAUSE	I NEED A MOMENT TO REFLECT	
[NOTHING]	DIED ?	MY INTEREST IN YOU DIED :̈
MISS YOU	I WANT TO GET BACK TOGETHER	I SAW THAT YOU'RE HAPPY

IS THIS A DEAL BREAKER?

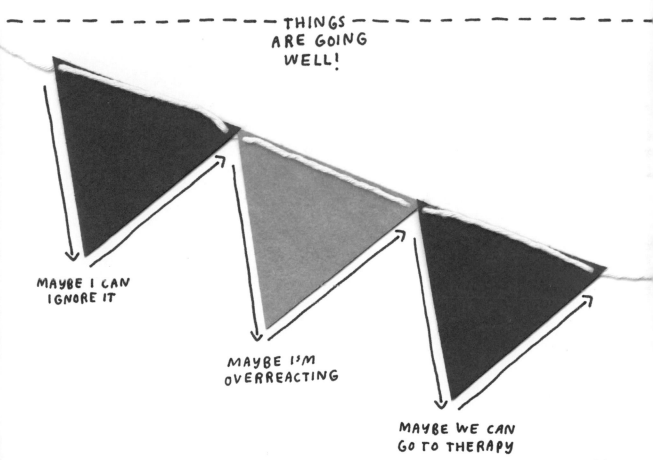

THINGS ARE GOING WELL!

MAYBE I CAN IGNORE IT

MAYBE I'M OVERREACTING

MAYBE WE CAN GO TO THERAPY

IS THIS A
GOOD FIT?

JOB INTERVIEW

DATING

APARTMENT HUNTING

IS MY OUTFIT OK?

OFFER TO COMMIT RIGHT AWAY

EXPECT THEM TO GOOGLE YOU

DOESN'T LOOK LIKE THE PHOTOS

CAN YOU HANDLE
MY HANG-UPS?

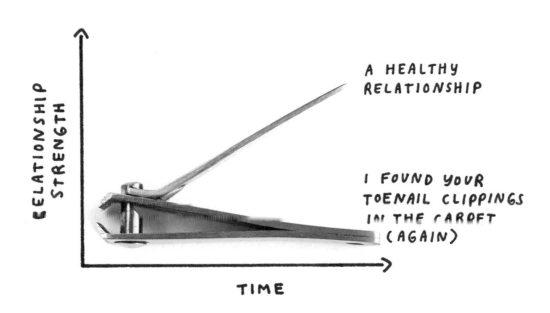

RELATIONSHIP STRENGTH

A HEALTHY
RELATIONSHIP

I FOUND YOUR
TOENAIL CLIPPINGS
IN THE CARPET
(AGAIN)

TIME

AM I A BAD FRIEND?

A QUIZ

YOUR FRIEND
GETS GOOD NEWS
(LIKE, *really* GOOD)

↓

HOW DO
YOU FEEL?

IF I'M BEING
HONEST, I FEEL
PRETTY JEALOUS—
IT'S SOMETHING
I'VE WANTED
FOR SO LONG

SOOOOOOO
HAPPY FOR
THEM!!!!

↑

OK, OK

↑

...and? ⟶

WHICH F·R·I·E·N·D AM I?

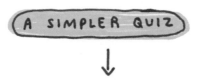

↓

PICK A VOCAL FREQUENCY
THAT RESONATES WITH YOU

IF YOU HAVE A PROBLEM WITH THE LEVEL OF
SCIENTIFIC ACCURACY OF THIS QUIZ, YOU'RE ROSS

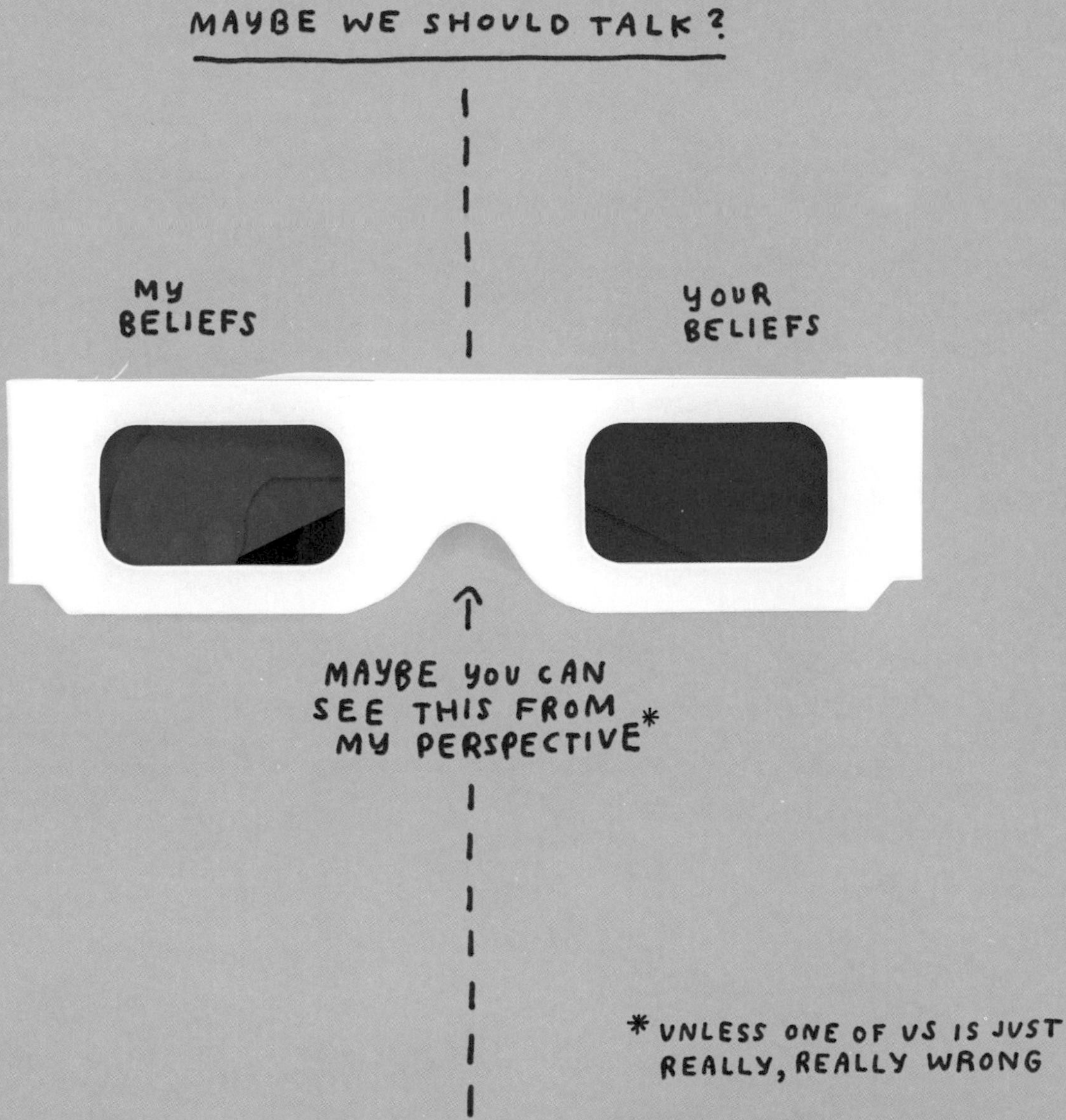
MAYBE WE SHOULD TALK?
MY BELIEFS
YOUR BELIEFS
MAYBE YOU CAN SEE THIS FROM MY PERSPECTIVE*
* UNLESS ONE OF US IS JUST REALLY, REALLY WRONG

EXCITED FOR THE HOLIDAYS?

DESIRE TO BE WITH FAMILY

HOLIDAY SEASON

TIME

WILL PARENTHOOD CHANGE EVERYTHING?

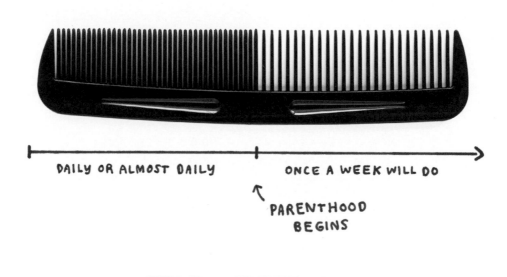

DAILY OR ALMOST DAILY

ONCE A WEEK WILL DO

↑ PARENTHOOD BEGINS

(HAIR WASHING FREQUENCY)

WELL, OK, I MEANT *everything*

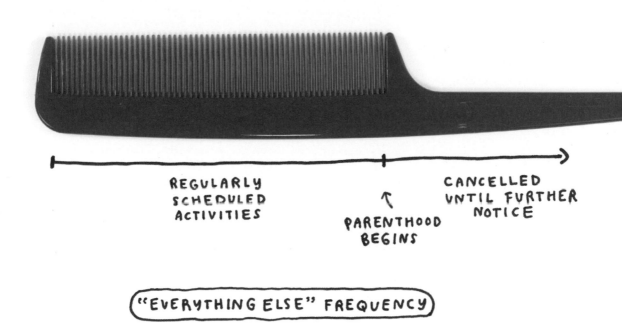

REGULARLY SCHEDULED ACTIVITIES

PARENTHOOD BEGINS

CANCELLED UNTIL FURTHER NOTICE

"EVERYTHING ELSE" FREQUENCY

OVERTHINKING

the Small Stuff

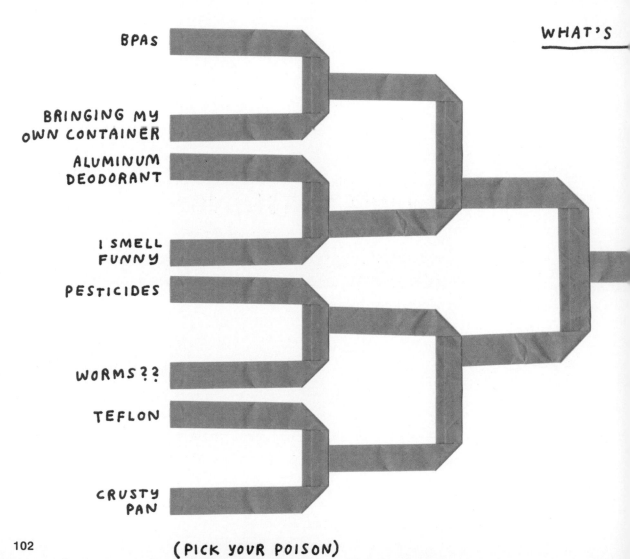

BPAS

BRINGING MY OWN CONTAINER

ALUMINUM DEODORANT

I SMELL FUNNY

PESTICIDES

WORMS??

TEFLON

CRUSTY PAN

102

(PICK YOUR POISON)

WORSE?

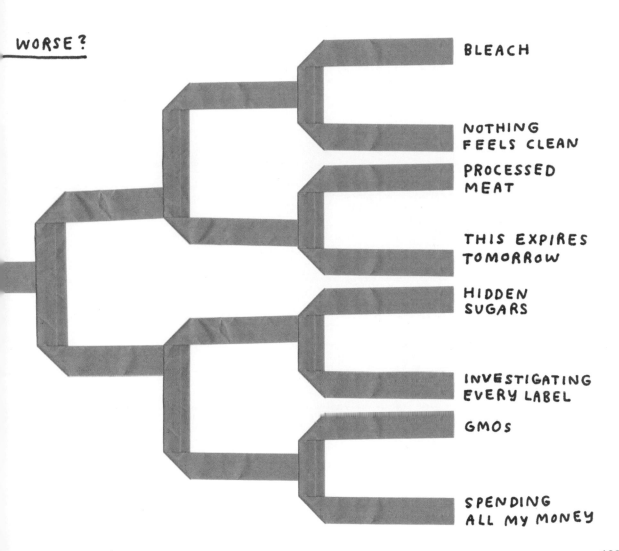

BLEACH

NOTHING FEELS CLEAN

PROCESSED MEAT

THIS EXPIRES TOMORROW

HIDDEN SUGARS

INVESTIGATING EVERY LABEL

GMOS

SPENDING ALL MY MONEY

IS IT TOO EARLY TO PLAN MY HALLOWEEN COSTUME?

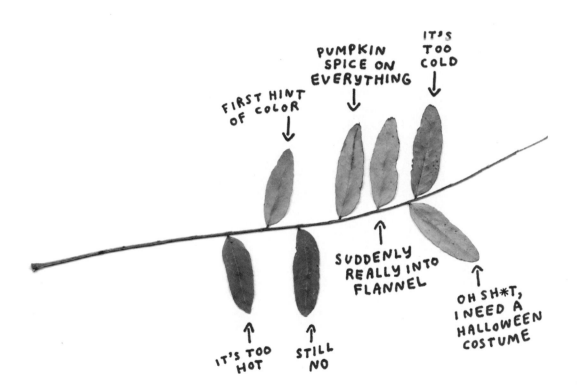

FIRST HINT OF COLOR

PUMPKIN SPICE ON EVERYTHING

IT'S TOO COLD

IT'S TOO HOT

STILL NO

SUDDENLY REALLY INTO FLANNEL

OH SH*T, I NEED A HALLOWEEN COSTUME

CAN I MAKE IT THROUGH
ANOTHER HARSH WINTER?

SELF-FULFILLMENT NEEDS
A HAT WITH A BALL ON IT

ESTEEM NEEDS
A WARM COAT THAT
LOOKS NICE

COZY NEEDS
MOODY MUSIC,
SOFT BLANKETS,
TWINKLE LIGHTS,
HOT CHOCOLATE,
HOT CIDER,
HOT TODDY

SAFETY NEEDS
THE IDEAL
SEAT AT MY
FAVORITE CAFÉ

A HIERARCHY
OF WINTER COPING
MECHANISMS

105

WILL I EVER USE THE MATH I LEARNED IN SCHOOL?

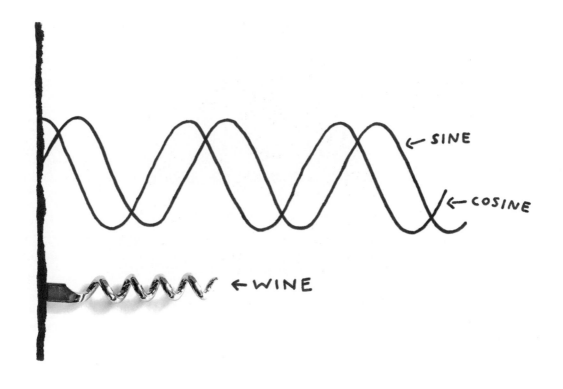

← SINE

← COSINE

← WINE

WILL I EVER USE THE MATH
I LEARNED IN "MEAN GIRLS"?

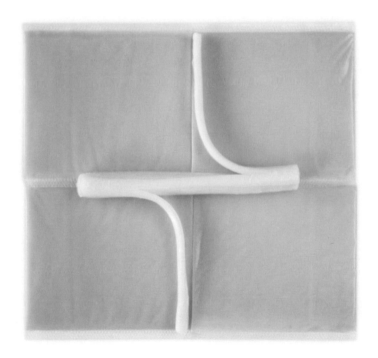

↿ MY CHEESE LIMIT DOES NOT EXIST ↾

IS MY HAIRCUT AWFUL?

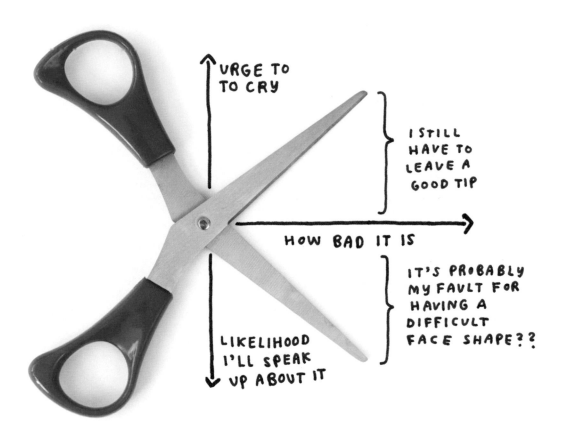

URGE TO TO CRY

I STILL HAVE TO LEAVE A GOOD TIP

HOW BAD IT IS

IT'S PROBABLY MY FAULT FOR HAVING A DIFFICULT FACE SHAPE??

LIKELIHOOD I'LL SPEAK UP ABOUT IT

HOW MUCH DO I TIP FOR THIS?

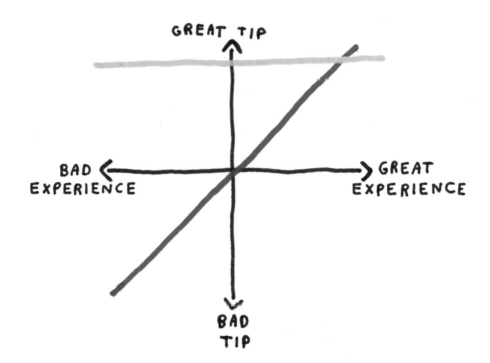

GREAT TIP

BAD EXPERIENCE

GREAT EXPERIENCE

BAD TIP

● SOME PEOPLE   ○ ANYONE WHO HAS EVER WORKED IN THE SERVICE INDUSTRY (IN THE U.S.)

DOES EVERYWHERE IN L.A. TAKE TWENTY MINUTES?

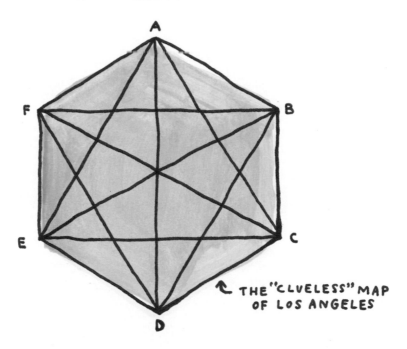

↖ THE "CLUELESS" MAP OF LOS ANGELES

AB 20 MINUTES   BC 20 MINUTES   CE 20 MINUTES
AC 20 MINUTES   BD 20 MINUTES   CF 20 MINUTES
AD 20 MINUTES   BE 20 MINUTES   DE 20 MINUTES
AE 20 MINUTES   BF 20 MINUTES   DF 20 MINUTES
AF 20 MINUTES   CD 20 MINUTES   EF 20 MINUTES

WHY AM I
always LATE?

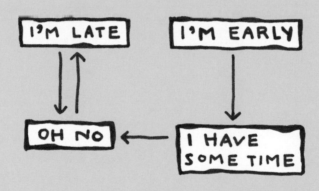

WHY DON'T I BIKE MORE OFTEN?

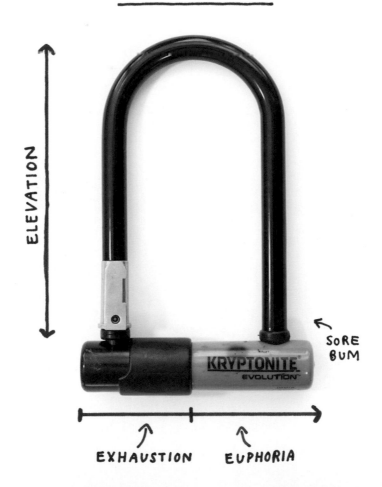

ELEVATION

SORE BUM

EXHAUSTION   EUPHORIA

WHAT'S WRONG
WITH MY CAR?

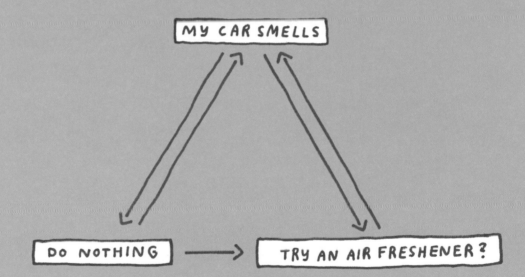

CAN I WORK FROM THIS COFFEE SHOP?

THINGS I NEED FROM A COFFEE SHOP

No. 1 FAST WI-FI

No. 2 A GOOD BATHROOM

AM I SPENDING ENOUGH
TIME IN NATURE?

TIME SPENT
OUTSIDE →

JOY

OK, THAT'S
ENOUGH

WHAT CAN I LEARN
FROM THE OUTDOORS?

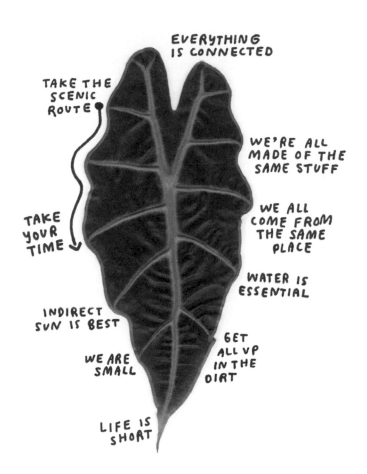

EVERYTHING IS CONNECTED

TAKE THE SCENIC ROUTE

WE'RE ALL MADE OF THE SAME STUFF

WE ALL COME FROM THE SAME PLACE

TAKE YOUR TIME

WATER IS ESSENTIAL

INDIRECT SUN IS BEST

GET ALL UP IN THE DIRT

WE ARE SMALL

LIFE IS SHORT

OVERTHINKING

the Big Stuff

HOW DO I FIND
A GOOD DOCTOR?

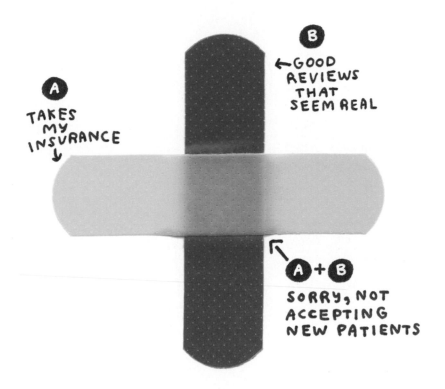

B
← GOOD REVIEWS THAT SEEM REAL

A
TAKES MY INSURANCE ↓

A + B
SORRY, NOT ACCEPTING NEW PATIENTS

WHAT IF THERE REALLY is SOMETHING WRONG WITH ME?

PROS	CONS
I WAS RIGHT	THERE'S SOMETHING WRONG WITH ME
THIS EXPLAINS ALL MY PROBLEMS	
I'M NOT A HYPOCHONDRIAC	
THERE MIGHT BE WAYS TO MANAGE IT	
PEOPLE WILL UNDERSTAND NOW	

HOW DO I STAY CALM?

BREATHE OUT

FOCUS ON YOUR BREATH

BREATHE IN

AM I DOING ENOUGH?

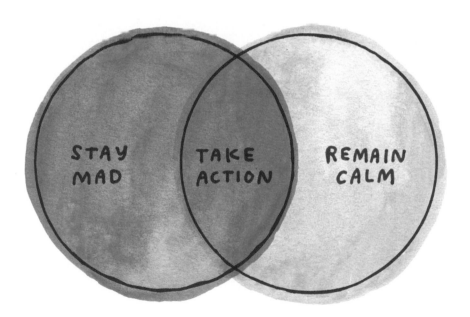

DO I REALLY NEED TO WORRY ABOUT CLIMATE CHANGE?

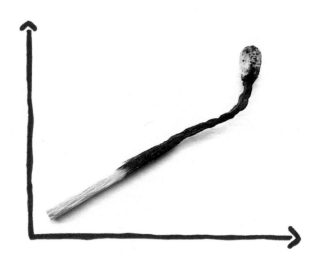

WEATHER SEVERITY

EARTH'S TEMPERATURE

WHAT IF IT'S TOO LATE?

DO

WORK
TOGETHER
TO MAKE
CHANGE

DON'T

BECOME
PARALYZED
BY DESPAIR

WHAT CAN I
DO TO HELP?

A NEW
LIFE

A LOST
LIFE

↑
SHOW UP,
BRING FOOD

WHAT IS THERE TO BE GRATEFUL FOR?

THERE'S ALWAYS SOMETHING						
LIFE	LIFE	LIFE	KETTLE CORN	LIFE	LIFE	SELTZER
LIFE	LIFE	LOVE	LIFE	LIFE	HEALTH	LIFE
WATER	LIFE	FAMILY	LIFE	MOVE-MENT	LIFE	THE WOODS
MUSIC	DANCE	LIFE	FRIENDS	HOT TEA	CLEAN AIR	A HOME
LAUGH-TER	THE SUN	LIFE				

IS THIS
OBVIOUS
YET?

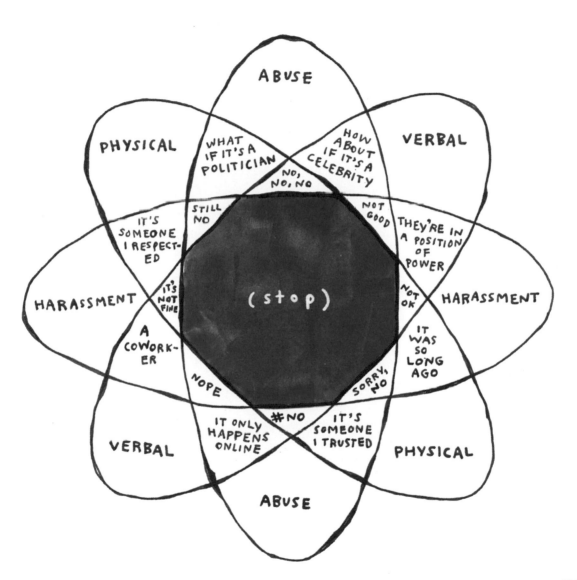

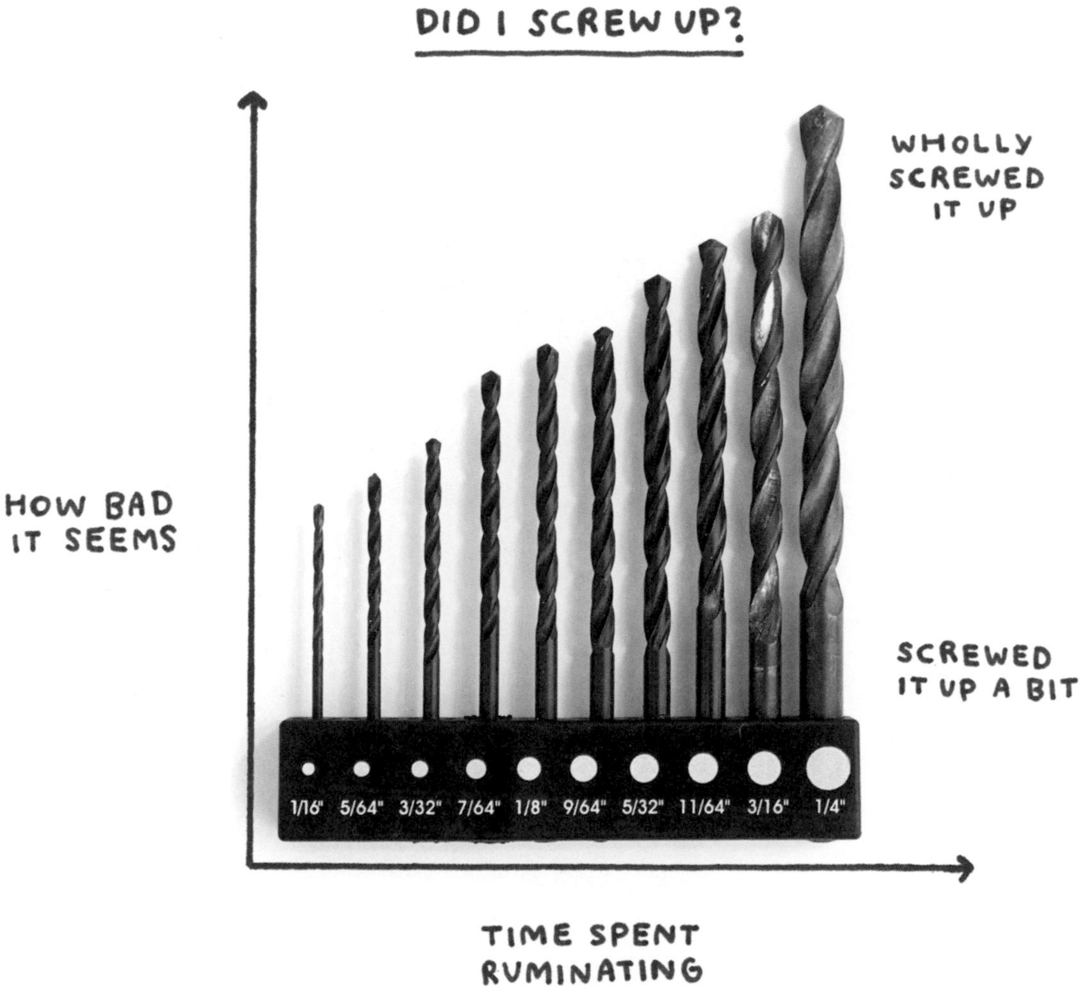

DID I SCREW UP?

WHOLLY
SCREWED
IT UP

SCREWED
IT UP A BIT

HOW BAD
IT SEEMS

1/16" 5/64" 3/32" 7/64" 1/8" 9/64" 5/32" 11/64" 3/16" 1/4"

TIME SPENT
RUMINATING

SHOULD I GIVE MYSELF A BREAK?

WHY AM I
SO HARD ON
MYSELF?

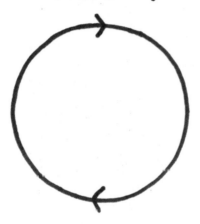

I AM TOO
HARD ON
MYSELF

WHAT WOULD THE BEATLES DO?

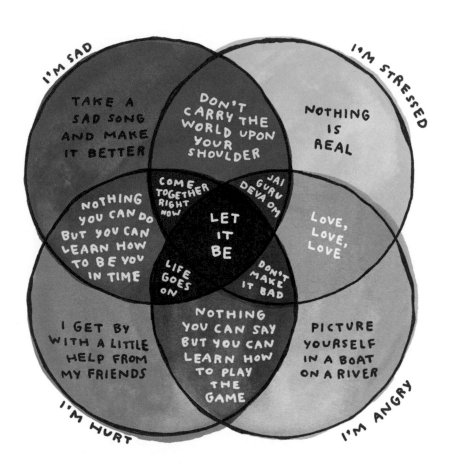

HOW DO YOU MEASURE,*
MEASURE A YEAR?

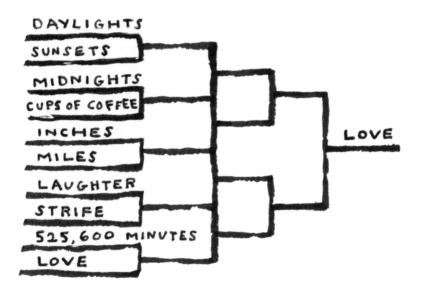

DAYLIGHTS
SUNSETS
MIDNIGHTS
CUPS OF COFFEE
INCHES
MILES
LAUGHTER
STRIFE
525,600 MINUTES
LOVE

LOVE

*ACCORDING TO "RENT"

133

WILL IT
_____
BE OK?
_____

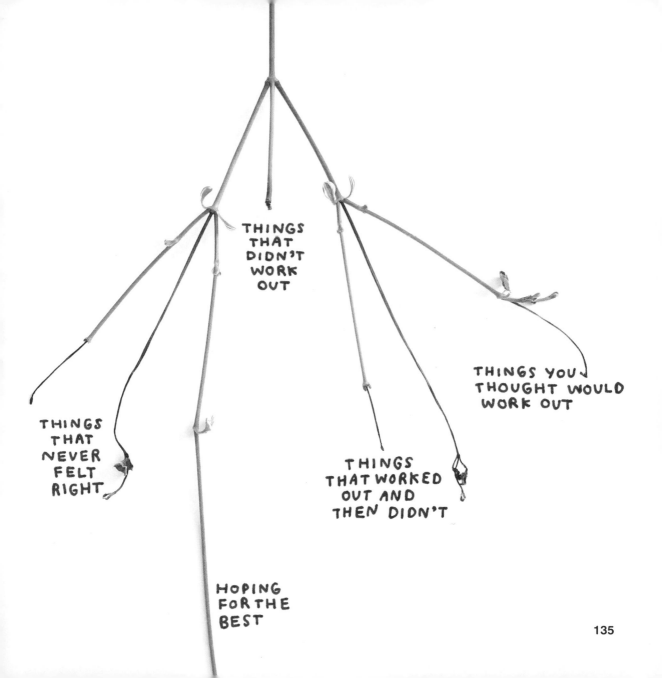

THINGS
THAT
DIDN'T
WORK
OUT

THINGS YOU
THOUGHT WOULD
WORK OUT

THINGS
THAT
NEVER
FELT
RIGHT

THINGS
THAT WORKED
OUT AND
THEN DIDN'T

HOPING
FOR THE
BEST

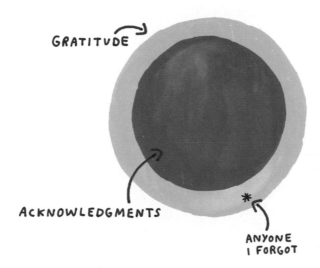

GRATITUDE

ACKNOWLEDGMENTS

ANYONE
I FORGOT

I'm so grateful for the opportunity to send this book out into the world, and for everyone who had a part in making that happen.

A big thank-you to my editor, Deanne Katz, and the rest of the team at Chronicle Books for taking on and shaping this project.

Thank you to Vanessa Hope Schneider for playing friend-agent and encouraging me to do this long before I had the chutzpah.

Thank you to so many Jessicas: Saia, for letting me pitch "made-up charts" for actual money; Misener, for hiring me to make charts as a real job; and Hische, for making the first chart I ever loved.

Thank you to Jason Kottke, Nathan Pyle, Adam J. Kurtz, Caroline Siede, Champ Teepagorn, and so many more of my art and internet heroes for the unexpected support and for finding my work worthy of sharing with others.

Thank you to Tim, Margaret, and Rob for literally keeping my head on straight.

Thank you to my family for the love and support. Thank you to my dad, José, for sparking my interest in the patterns and math behind everyday things, and my mom, Omaira, for being my biggest fan. Alexa, play "Las Mañanitas."

Most of all, thank you to Lenny for the infinite support, positivity, and dance breaks. I'm sorry about the mess.

MUCH DO I TIP FOR THIS? WHY AM I ALWAYS LATE? HOW'S MY
NG TO REGRET THIS? SHOULD I MOVE ACROSS THE COUNTRY? WHICH
E IN NATURE? HAS THIS EVER HAPPENED TO YOU? CAN I WORK FROM
T'S WRONG WITH MY CAR? WHAT'S THAT SMELL? ARE AIR FRESHENE
INSURANCE? WHAT CAN I DO TO HELP? IS THAT A BAD QUESTION? H
NG TO LOOK TERRIBLE? SHOULD I START MEDITATING? IS THIS A PAR
K SOMETHING? SHOULD I BUY THIS? DO I NEED TO DECLUTTER MY HOM
I NEED TO CANCEL MY CREDIT CARDS? WHAT SHOULD WE LISTEN T
D WINE? CAN I BRING IT TO A PARTY? SHOULD I GRAB SOME KALE
EL ILL? AM I GOOD AT MY JOB? IS THIS IMPOSTER SYNDROME? AM
I STILL HAVE A JOB? WHAT DID THAT EMAIL MEAN? HOW SHOULD
UT ME? WHICH TOTE BAG SHOULD I USE? WHICH GROCERY S
TY? HOW DO I MAKE SMALL TALK? DO WE HAVE ANYTHING BET
I SPELL THAT RIGHT? CORRECTLY? FURTHER OR FARTHER? AFF
ULD I READ MY BOOK IN THE BATHTUB? SHOULD I LEND YOU
THERE REALLY IS SOMETHING WRONG WITH ME? WHAT IF I WAS
T IMPORTANT TO DISAGREE ON BIG ISSUES EVEN IF YOU CAN'T
N DO I STAY CALM? WILL IT BE OK? WILL I EVER USE THE MATH
ICH WHITE PAINT SHOULD I USE? DO I HAVE TOO MANY PLANT
RENTHOOD CHANGE EVERYTHING? HAS ANYONE SEEN MY SUNG
AT AM I FORGETTING? STILL OR SPARKLING? AM I EATING TO
RE? DOES THIS NEED MORE BUTTER? CAN I CLIP MY TOENAILS H
GE OF OUR RELATIONSHIP? WHAT DID THAT TEXT MEAN? IS
HERE TO BE GRATEFUL FOR? HOW DO YOU MEASURE, MEASURE
MODELING THE BATHROOM MYSELF? IS IT AS EASY AS IT LOO
CREDIT CARDS OR SHOULD I TRY TO FIND IT THIS TIME? AM I F
IR BIRTHDAY? WHY DO PEOPLE LOVE CAMPING SO MUCH? WHA
IP WITHOUT CAUSING PERMANENT DAMAGE? WHAT SHOULD
.A. TAKE TWENTY MINUTES? SHOULD I TOUCH THIS DOOR H
TANDING DESK MAKE A DIFFERENCE? IS THIS TOO MANY EXCL
UGH? SHOULD I GO OUT? AM I TOO OLD? SHOULD I STAY I
THIS BOOK MAKE ME SOUND NEUROTIC? IS THERE A WORD F